Introducción a los padres

We Both Read es la primera serie de libros diseñada para invitar a padres e hijos a compartir la lectura de un cuento, por turnos y en voz alta. Esta "lectura compartida" —que se ha desarrollado en conjunto con especialistas en primeras lecturas— invita a los padres a leer los textos más complejos en la página de la izquierda. Luego, les toca a los niños leer las páginas de la derecha, que contienen textos más sencillos, escritos específicamente para primeros lectores.

Leer en voz alta es una de las actividades más importantes que los padres comparten con sus hijos para ayudarlos a desarrollar la lectura. Sin embargo, *We Both Read* no es solo leerle *a* un niño, sino que les permite a los padres leer *con* el niño. *We Both Read* es más poderoso y efectivo porque combina dos elementos claves del aprendizaje: "demostración" (el padre lee) y "aplicación" (el niño lee). El resultado no es solo que el niño aprende a leer más rápido, ¡sino que ambos disfrutan y se enriquecen con esta experiencia!

Sería más útil si usted lee el libro completo y en voz alta la primera vez, y luego invita a su niño a participar en una segunda lectura. En algunos libros, las palabras más difíciles se presentan por primera vez en **negritas** en el texto del padre. Señalar o hablar sobre estas palabras ayudará a su niño a familiarizarse con ellas y a ampliar su vocabulario. También notará que el ícono "lee el padre" ☺ precede el texto del padre y el ícono "lee el niño" ☺ precede el texto del niño.

Lo invitamos a compartir y a relacionarse con su niño mientras leen el libro juntos. Si su hijo tiene dificultad, usted puede mencionar algunas cosas que lo ayuden. "Decir cada sonido" es bueno, pero puede que esto no funcione con todas las palabras. Los niños pueden hallar pistas en las palabras del cuento, en el contexto de las oraciones e incluso de las imágenes. Algunos cuentos incluyen patrones y rimas que los ayudarán. También le podría ser útil a su niño tocar las palabras con su dedo mientras leen para conectar mejor el sonido de la voz con la palabra impresa.

¡Al compartir los libros de *We Both Read*, usted y su hijo vivirán juntos la fascinante aventura de la lectura! Es una manera divertida y fácil de animar y ayudar a su niño a leer —¡y una maravillosa manera de preparar a su niño para disfrutar de la lectura durante toda su vida!

Parent's Introduction

We Both Read is the first series of books designed to invite parents and children to share the reading of a story by taking turns reading aloud. This "shared reading" innovation, which was developed with reading education specialists, invites parents to read the more complex text and storyline on the left-hand pages. Then, children can be encouraged to read the right-hand pages, which feature less complex text and storyline, specifically written for the beginning reader.

Reading aloud is one of the most important activities parents can share with their child to assist in his or her reading development. However, *We Both Read* goes beyond reading *to* a child and allows parents to share the reading *with* a child. *We Both Read* is so powerful and effective because it combines two key elements in learning: "modeling" (the parent reads) and "doing" (the child reads). The result is not only faster reading development for the child, but a much more enjoyable and enriching experience for both!

You may find it helpful to read the entire book aloud yourself the first time, then invite your child to participate in the second reading. In some books, a few more difficult words will first be introduced in the parent's text, distinguished with **bold lettering**. Pointing out, and even discussing, these words will help familiarize your child with them and help to build your child's vocabulary. Also, note that a "talking parent" icon ☺ precedes the parent's text and a "talking child" icon ☺ precedes the child's text.

We encourage you to share and interact with your child as you read the book together. If your child is having difficulty, you might want to mention a few things to help him or her. "Sounding out" is good, but it will not work with all words. Children can pick up clues about the words they are reading from the story, the context of the sentence, or even the pictures. Some stories have rhyming patterns that might help. It might also help them to touch the words with their finger as they read, to better connect the voice sound and the printed word.

Sharing the *We Both Read* books together will engage you and your child in an interactive adventure in reading! It is a fun and easy way to encourage and help your child to read—and a wonderful way to start your child off on a lifetime of reading enjoyment!

About Pets
A We Both Read® Book
Level 1

Las mascotas
Un libro de *We Both Read*
Nivel 1

For Maggie, Toto, Squeaky, and Bree—my best friends.
Para Maggie, Toto, Squeaky y Bree: mis mejores amigos

English text Copyright © 2002 by Sindy McKay
Editorial and Production Services by Cambridge BrickHouse, Inc.
Spanish translation © 2014 by Treasure Bay, Inc.
All rights reserved

Use of photographs provided by Getty Images
© Copyright 2002

We Both Read™ is a registered trademark of Treasure Bay, Inc.

Published by
Treasure Bay, Inc.
P.O. Box 119
Novato, CA 94948 USA

Printed in Singapore

Library of Congress Control Number: 2014938418

ISBN-13: 978-1-60115-062-2

We Both Read® Books
Patent No. 5,957,693

Visit us online at:
www.webothread.com

PR 11-14

About Pets
Las mascotas

By Sindy McKay

Traducido por Yanitzia Canetti

TREASURE BAY

Dogs, cats, fish, birds, lizards, rats—**pets** are everywhere! They come in all different shapes, sizes and colors.

Perros, gatos, peces, pájaros, lagartos, ratas: ¡hay **mascotas** *dondequiera! Las hay de diferentes formas, tamaños y colores.*

🔊 **Pets** can be big.
Pets can be small.

*Las **mascotas** pueden ser grandes.*
Las mascotas pueden ser pequeñas.

Pets may have lots of nice fluffy fur or they may be silky-smooth and shiny. Some pets have scales and some have wings. There are pets with gills and pets with shells. Can you think of a pet that has a **shell**?

*Las mascotas pueden tener un pelaje grueso y mullido o pueden ser suaves, sedosas y brillantes. Algunas tienen escamas y otras tienen alas. Unas tienen aletas y otras, caparazones. ¿Te viene a la mente alguna con **caparazón**?*

Look at my turtle!
Turtles have a **shell**.

¡Mira mi tortuga!
*Las tortugas tienen **caparazón**.*

Pets have different needs. Birds need a cage to **sleep** in, but cats **sleep** anywhere they want to. A dog must be fed every day, but some snakes only eat once a week. Good pet owners know what's best for their pet.

*Las mascotas tienen diferentes necesidades. Los pájaros necesitan una jaula para **dormir**, pero los gatos duermen dondequiera. Los perros comen todos los días, pero algunas serpientes solo comen una vez a la semana. Los dueños saben qué es lo mejor para su mascota.*

Cats like to **sleep** in the sun.

*A los gatos les gusta **dormir** bajo el sol.*

 According to some sources, cats are the world's most popular pets. Maybe that's because cats are easy to care for. Cats don't seem to mind being left alone while their owners are away at school or work. They can **purr** while curled up in your lap.

*Según algunas fuentes, los gatos son las mascotas más populares del mundo. Tal vez sea porque son fáciles de cuidar. A los gatos no parece importarles que los dejen solos cuando sus dueños van a la escuela o al trabajo. Además pueden **ronronear** mientras se acurrucan en tu regazo.*

A cat has soft fur.
It may **purr** if you pet it.

El gato tiene un pelaje suave.
*Puede **ronronear** si lo acaricias.*

Some people say that dogs are the most popular pets in the world. That could be because there are so many different kinds of dogs to choose from. Or it might just be because a **puppy** is too doggone cute to resist!

*Algunas personas dicen que los perros son las mascotas más populares del mundo. Tal vez sea porque hay muchos tipos de perros para elegir. ¡O tal vez solo sea porque nadie podría resistirse a tener un lindo **cachorro**!*

A **puppy** is a lot of fun to play with!

¡Es muy divertido jugar con un cachorro!

Dogs and cats may be the two most common household pets, but there are many other animals that make great pets as well. Some other favorite four-legged friends are rats, hamsters, rabbits, guinea pigs, lizards, turtles, and pigs.

Puede que los perros y los gatos sean las dos mascotas más comunes para tener en casa, pero hay muchos otros animales que también son estupendas mascotas. Otros amiguitos de cuatro patas son las ratas, los hámsters, los conejos, los cobayas, los lagartos, las tortugas y los cerditos

This girl has a big pig for a pet.

Esta niña tiene un cerdito grande como mascota.

Not all pets have four legs. Many people choose birds as pets, while others might choose **fish** or one of several species of snakes.

*No todas las mascotas tienen cuatro patas. Muchas personas eligen aves como mascotas. Otras eligen **peces** o una de las diversas especies de serpientes.*

 **Fish** make good pets.
Cats like them, too!

*Los **peces** son buenas mascotas.*
¡A los gatos también les gustan!

15

Pet owners try to spend as much time as possible with their pets and many will **talk** to them the same way they talk to a good friend.

*Los dueños de mascotas tratan de pasar el mayor tiempo posible con ellas. A muchos les gusta **hablar** con su mascota de la misma forma que hablan con un buen amigo.*

Birds love to sing.
Some birds can even **talk**.

A las aves les gusta cantar.
Algunas aves pueden incluso
hablar.

17

 The variety of pets available is wonderful. But no matter what animal you choose as a pet, it must be well cared for and loved. It can even travel with you in a **car**.

*La variedad de mascotas a tu alcance es maravilosa. Pero no importa qué animal elijas como mascota, lo importante es que lo quieras y lo cuides bien. Puede incluso viajar contigo en el **carro**.*

This dog loves to ride in the **car**.

A este perro le encanta pasear en ***carro****.*

 Owning a pet is a big responsibility. An animal that has become a pet cannot take care of itself. It is the owner's responsibility to provide the right food for their pet along with plenty of fresh water to **drink**.

*Tener una mascota es una gran responsabilidad. Un animal que se vuelve mascota no se puede cuidar a sí mismo. Es responsabilidad del dueño darle la comida adecuada y mucha agua fresca para **beber**.*

Oh, no! That water is not to **drink**.

¡Oh, no! ¡Esa agua no es para beber!

Some pets like to eat the same **food** we eat. However, feeding "people food" to a pet is not a good idea. Pets need to eat special food that has been made just for them.

*A algunas mascotas les gusta la misma **comida** que a nosotros. Pero no es bueno darles "comida de personas". Necesitan una comida especial que ha sido elaborada específicamente para ellas.*

Some dogs beg for **food**.
Some kids beg for food, too!

*Algunos perritos piden **comida**.*
¡Algunos niñitos piden comida
también!

23

 Another important aspect of caring for a pet is making sure it gets enough exercise. Goldfish can take care of getting their own exercise, but cats enjoy playing with toys. Just rolling a ball of yarn across the room can keep a cat busy for a long time.

Otra manera de cuidar a una mascota es asegurarse de que esta haga suficiente ejercicio. Un pez hace sus propios ejercicios, pero a los gatos les encantan los juguetes. Si haces rodar una bola de estambre, un gato estará entretenido por buen rato.

Dogs love to play.
They love to run and jump.

A los perros les encanta jugar.
Les encanta correr y saltar.

Regular visits to the veterinarian will help assure that your pet stays healthy. A veterinarian can advise you on the right diet and exercise to keep your pet **happy** and give any shots or medicine to prevent disease.

*Para asegurarte de que tu mascota esté saludable, es importante visitar regularmente al veterinario. Un veterinario puede recomendarte la dieta y los ejercicios adecuados para mantener a tu mascota **feliz** y darle cualquier vacuna o medicina para prevenir enfermedades.*

A well pet is a **happy** pet.

*Una mascota sana es una mascota **feliz**.*

27

 Most pets require some kind of bathing and grooming. Many need regular haircuts and **baths**, and some may need to have their nails clipped and their teeth brushed.

*La mayoría de las mascotas requieren que las bañen y las arreglen. Muchas necesitan frecuentes cortes de pelo y **baños**, y algunas podrían necesitar tener sus uñas recortadas y sus dientes cepillados.*

This big dog takes **baths** in a big tub.

*Este perro grande toma **baños** en una tina grande.*

Having a place to call home is important for pets. Birds need a large, clean cage of their very own. Fish **live** in an aquarium. Many reptiles and snakes need a special enclosure with a heater to keep their body temperatures steady.

Para las mascotas es importante tener un hogar. Las aves necesitan su propia jaula, limpia y grande. El pez **vive** *en una pecera. Muchos lagartos y serpientes necesitan un espacio con un calefactor que mantenga estable la temperatura de sus cuerpos.*

 This dog loves to **live** in a house!

*Este perro **vive** en una casa. ¡Y le encanta!*

One of the most important things a pet needs to grow healthy and happy is the time and affection of its owner.

Una de las cosas más importantes que necesita una mascota para que crezca sana y feliz es la dedicación y el cariño de su dueño.

Give your pet a big hug.
That makes it feel good.

Dale a tu mascota un gran abrazo.
Eso la hace sentir bien.

If you are thinking of getting a new pet, it's a good idea to spend some time deciding what kind of pet is right for you. Consider how much time you have to spend with the animal and how much money you are willing to spend on its care and upkeep.

Si estás pensando en tener una nueva mascota, sería bueno que dedicaras un tiempo a pensar qué tipo de mascota es la mejor para ti. Toma en cuenta cuánto tiempo le puedes dedicar al animal y cuánto dinero puedes gastar en su cuidado y mantenimiento.

 A dog or cat makes a good pet. So does a frog.

Un perro o un gato son buenas mascotas. Al igual que una rana.

Few things are **cuter** than a puppy, but a puppy can be a real handful! You might want to think about choosing an older animal that's already been trained. If you're not going to be home much, consider getting two pets so they can keep each other company.

*Pocas cosas son **más bonitas** que un cachorro, ¡pero puede darte problemas! Tal vez debas considerar un animal mayor, que ya esté entrenado. Si tú no vas a estar mucho tiempo en casa, considera dos mascotas para que se acompañen mutuamente.*

One dog is cute.
Two dogs are **cuter**!

Un perro es bonito.
*¡Dos perros son **más bonitos**!*

It doesn't take long for a pet to become part of our lives, and soon we wonder how we ever got along without them. They join us at work and at **play**. They cheer us up when we're sad and share our joy when we're feeling happy.

*No se necesita mucho tiempo para que una mascota forme parte de nuestra vida, y pronto nos preguntamos cómo hemos podido estar sin ella. Ellas trabajan y **juegan** con nosotros. Nos animan cuando estamos tristes y comparten nuestra alegría cuando nos sentimos felices.*

They **play** with us.
They even sing with us.

*Ellas **juegan** con nosotros.*
Incluso cantan con nosotros.

 If we give our pets what they need, they will give back to us love and devotion and laughter.

Si le damos a nuestras mascotas lo que necesitan, nos devolverán amor, devoción y risa.

 A pet is a very nice thing.

Una mascota es algo muy bueno.

If you liked **About Pets,** here is another
We Both Read® book you are sure to enjoy!
*Si te gustó **Las mascotas,** ¡seguramente disfrutarás
este otro libro de la serie We Both Read®!*

Amazing Eggs
Huevos asombrosos

Learn about some fascinating animals and
how they begin their lives—hatching from
an egg!

*Aprende sobre algunos animales fascinantes,
¡y cómo estos comenzaron sus vidas al salir
de un huevo!*

To see all the We Both Read books that are available,
just go online to **www.WeBothRead.com**.

*Para ver todos los libros disponibles de la serie We Both Read®,
visita nuestra página web:* **www.WeBothRead.com.**